D ELANEY
S TREET
P RESS

Graduation
and
Beyond

Graduation
and
Beyond

A Concise Guide for
Life After Graduation

by Dr. Criswell Freeman

DELANEY STREET PRESS
Nashville, TN: (800) 256-8584

ISBN 1-58334-068-8

The ideas expressed in this book are not, in all cases, exact quotations, as some have been edited for clarity and brevity. In all cases, the author has attempted to maintain the speaker's original intent. In some cases, material for this book was obtained from secondary sources, primarily print media. While every effort was made to ensure the accuracy of these sources, the accuracy cannot be guaranteed. For additions, deletions, corrections or clarifications in future editions of this text, please write DELANEY STREET PRESS.

Printed in the United States of America
Cover Design by Bart Dawson
Layout by Swan Lake Communications,
Jackson, Mississippi

1 2 3 4 5 6 7 8 9 10 • 00 01 02 03 04 05 06

ACKNOWLEDGMENTS

The author gratefully acknowledges the helpful support of Angela Beasley Freeman, Dick and Mary Freeman, Mary Susan Freeman, Jim Gallery, and the entire team of professionals at DELANEY STREET PRESS and WALNUT GROVE PRESS.

For the Faculty and Staff of
Vanderbilt University
and for the Members
of the Class of 1976

Table of Contents

Introduction

Because you're reading a book with the word "Graduation" in its title, it's likely that *you* have recently graduated from something. If so, please accept a hearty congratulations! You've earned it.

Now, with school a not-so-distant memory, you are faced with a multitude of decisions: where to live, where to work, what to do about your personal relationships. In short, you are faced with important choices that will have a profound impact on you and your loved ones. This book is intended to help.

You hold in your hand a book packed with great ideas. On the pages that follow, some of history's best thinkers share insights that can enhance the quality of your life now and for years to come. As a way of organizing these thoughts, I have divided this text into nine chapters, each addressing an overriding principle.

These nine principles are powerful tools that have worked for others and will work for you — so use them, pass them on, and while you're at it, have a wonderful life.

PRINCIPLE #1

Lifetime Learning

Okay, school is out, and the last thing you want to do is read. After all, you've had your nose in a book and your eyes glued to a computer screen for years. But, it's important to realize that formal schooling constitutes the beginning, not the end, of your education. Now comes the exciting part.

With the sheepskin safely signed and framed, you are suddenly free to study the things that interest *you*, and you're free to study them on your own timetable.

So put down the TV clicker, pick up a book, and let the lifetime learning begin! Because graduation may be over, but here in the real world, school is always in session.

No man ever became wise
by chance.

Seneca

Learning is not attained
by chance. It must be searched
for with ardor and attended
to with diligence.

Abigail Adams

It is what we think we know
that prevents us
from learning.

Claude Bernard

It's what you know after you know it all that counts.

HARRY TRUMAN

I am still learning.

MICHELANGELO'S MOTTO

The years have much
to teach which the days
never know.

Ralph Waldo Emerson

A man, though wise,
should never be ashamed
of learning more.

Sophocles

I learn from anyone,
but I do not stop at that.
I go on trying to learn
from myself.

Zane Grey

The purpose of learning
　　is growth, and our minds,
unlike our bodies, can continue
to grow as we continue to live.
Mortimer Adler

To learn is a natural
　　pleasure not confined
　　to philosophers, but
　　common to all men.
Aristotle

In a time of drastic change,
　　it is the learners who
　　inherit the future.
Eric Hoffer

There are some things
you can best learn in calm,
and some in storm.

Willa Cather

The illiterate of the future
will not be the person who
cannot read. It will be the
person who does not
know how to learn.

Alvin Toffler

A man should never stop
learning, even on his last day.

Maimonides

The excitement of learning
separates youth from old age.
As long as you're learning
you're not old.

Rosalyn Sussman Yalow

Never stop learning.
It keeps you young.

Patty Berg

The man who is too old
to learn was probably
always too old to learn.

Henry S. Haskins

Anyone who
stops learning
is old, whether
at twenty
or eighty.

HENRY FORD

In Summary: Five Tips for Lifetime Learning

- If you don't already have a card from the local public library, get one...and use it.

- Pick a favorite subject and vow to become an authority in your spare time. You'll be surprised how quickly you can become an expert if you apply yourself.

- Start your own personal library and begin stocking it with the very best books in your areas of interest.

- Continue to study English grammar. You'll need it for the rest of your life.

- Begin planning a big vacation to an interesting place, even if you can't take the trip for several years. Travel expands the mind.

Principle #2

Embracing Change

Now that you've graduated, you may be settling into a new job. If so, you're probably a little apprehensive, and who wouldn't be? After all, leaving school and starting work can be quite a change. Well, get used to it. Like it or not, change is a constant fact of life, so you might as well learn to embrace it.

Anne Morrow Lindbergh observed, "Only in growth, reform, and change, paradoxically enough, is true security to be found." Your world is changing more rapidly than ever, and it's up to you to adapt to those changes. Here's how.

Even if you're on the right
track, you'll get run over if
you sit there long enough.
Will Rogers

The main dangers in this life
are the people who want to
change everything —
or nothing.
Nancy Astor

The horizon leans forward,
offering you space to place
new steps of change.
Maya Angelou

When you're green
you're growing;
when you're ripe
you rot.

RAY KROC

Ask the God who made
you to keep remaking you.
Norman Vincent Peale

We must change
in order to survive.
Pearl Bailey

People wish to be settled,
but it is only as far as they are
unsettled that there is any
hope for them.
Ralph Waldo Emerson

Where we stand
is not as important
as the direction
in which we
are moving.

OLIVER WENDELL HOLMES, JR.

To keep our
faces toward change
and behave like free
spirits in the
presence of fate
is strength
undefeatable.

HELEN KELLER

Weep not that the world
changes — did it keep a stable,
changeless state, it were cause
indeed to weep.

William C. Bryant

Very often a change of self
is needed more than
a change of scene.

A. C. Benson

Only I can change my life.
No one can do it for me.

Carol Burnett

We must adjust to
    changing times and still
      hold to unchanging
        principles.

Jimmy Carter

I wanted to change the
world. But I have found that
    the only thing one can be
    sure of changing is oneself.

Aldous Huxley

Change your thoughts,
    and you change your world.

Norman Vincent Peale

There is no good reason
why we should not develop
and change until the last
day we live.

Karen Horney

One change leaves the way
open for the introduction
of others.

Niccolo Machiavelli

To live is to change, and
to be perfect is to have
changed often.

John Henry Newman

All changes, even the most
longed for, have their
melancholy; for what
we leave behind is a part of
ourselves; we must die to one
life before we can enter
into another!

Gail Sheehy

Life is about not knowing,
having to change, taking the
moment and making the best
of it, without knowing what's
going to happen next.
Delicious ambiguity.

Gilda Radner

God, give us
the serenity
to accept what
cannot be changed;
Give us the courage
to change what should
be changed; Give us
the wisdom to
distinguish one
from the other.

REINHOLD NIEBUHR

In Summary: Five Tips for Embracing Change

- Assume that your current job will be out-of-date within a few years. Given today's world, that's a fairly safe bet.

- Don't be afraid to move to another city. You can always move home later, and the experience of living in another town will broaden your perspective.

- Stay abreast of current technology. Remember: the library has computers and internet access, even if you don't.

- Don't be afraid to change jobs, or for that matter, careers. Much of what you have learned in one career will carry over into the next, especially that most useful talent known as "people skills."

- When unexpected disappointments occur, and they will, always look for the silver lining around the cloud of unwanted change.

PRINCIPLE #3

Hard Work

A third tool for success is the principle of hard work. It takes lots of effort to earn a degree, and it takes even more effort to become a success in postgraduate life.

General Colin Powell advised, "There are no secrets to success: Don't waste time looking for them. Success is the result of perfection, hard work, learning from failure, loyalty to those for whom you work, and persistence."

General Powell was correct. There is no secret shortcut to success, but there is one surefire path that leads inexorably to the top: hard work.

So find a job that you love and then give it your very best. That little extra effort can make a world of difference.

Work for your soul's sake.

EDGAR LEE MASTERS

Each man's talent is his call.
There is one direction in which
all doors are open to him.
Ralph Waldo Emerson

Think enthusiastically
about everything,
especially your work.
Norman Vincent Peale

Work joyfully and peacefully,
knowing that right thoughts
and right efforts will inevitably
bring about right results.
James Allen

People should tell their
children what life is about.
It's about work.
Lauren Bacall

When troubles arise,
wise men go to their work.
Elbert Hubbard

Diligence makes good luck.
Ben Franklin

Begin — to begin is
    half the work.

Ausonius

Be like a postage stamp:
    Stick to one thing
    'til you get there.

Josh Billings

It is easier to do a job right
    than to explain why
    you didn't.

Martin Van Buren

The more I want to get
something done,
the less I call it work.

Richard Bach

Nothing is really work
unless you would rather be
doing something else.

James Matthew Barrie

Luck? I've never depended
on it and I'm afraid of people
who do. Luck to me is something else: Hard work — and
realizing what is opportunity
and what isn't.

Lucille Ball

Do your work with your
whole heart, and you
will succeed — there is
so little competition.

Elbert Hubbard

I've always believed
that if you put in the work,
the results will come.

Michael Jordan

If my life had been made up
of eight-hour days, I do not
believe I could have
accomplished a great deal.

Thomas Edison

Like what you do.
If you don't like it,
do something else.

PAUL HARVEY

The reward of a thing well done is to have done it.

RALPH WALDO EMERSON

Talent is only a starting
   place in this business.
You've got to keep on
working that talent.

                Irving Berlin

Inspiration comes
   from working every day.

           Charles Baudelaire

Talent alone won't make you
a success. Neither will being
   in the right place at the
right time, unless you are
ready. The most important
question is: "Are you ready?"

             Johnny Carson

Believe in the Lord and he will do half the work — the last half.

CYRUS CURTIS

<u>In Summary: Five Tips for Building Your Career</u>

- On the job, give a little more effort than is expected. It's the best form of job security.

- At work, always have a smile on your face. Never complain or whine: Nobody ever complained his way to the top.

- Begin building a network of contacts inside and outside your company. Sometime before the end of your career, you'll be glad you did.

- Avoid the habit of making excuses. Do a good job and let your work speak for itself.

- Make every job a learning experience. Most jobs offer some form of continuing education. Take every opportunity to educate yourself.

Principle #4
Managing Time

School has a way of helping you manage your time. Classes are scheduled at regular times each week; homework is given out on a predictable basis; exams are announced weeks in advance. At school, if you show up on time, pay attention, and do the homework, you're almost guaranteed to pass. Unfortunately, life outside the ivy-covered halls of academia is not always so structured. After graduation, it's up to you, more than ever, to manage your time effectively.

If you prioritize your activities and avoid needless time-wasters, you'll be just fine. But if you fall victim to Old Man Procrastination, or if you turn into a couch potato, you'll make things very hard on yourself. So why not start life after graduation on a positive note by learning the habits of time management? After all, time is the fabric of life, and a life — especially yours — is too beautiful and precious to waste.

Do not act as if you had a thousand years to live.

MARCUS AURELIUS

One today
is worth two
tomorrows.

BEN FRANKLIN

Tomorrow's life is too late.
Live today.

Martial

Always remember that
the future comes one day
at a time.

Dean Acheson

Time is so precious that
God deals it out only
second by second.

Bishop Fulton J. Sheen

A wise person does at once,
what a fool does at last. Both
do the same thing; only at
different times.

John Dalberg Acton

All human power is
a compound of time
and patience.

Honoré de Balzac

Forget the past and live in
the present hour. Now is the
time to work, the time to fill.

Sarah Knowles Bolton

There is no royal road
 to anything. One thing at
 a time, and all things in
 succession. That which
 grows slowly endures.

J. G. Holland

There's time enough,
 but none to spare.

Charles W. Chesnutt

A schedule defends
from chaos and whim.
It is a net for catching days.
It is a scaffolding on which
a worker can stand and
labor with both hands
at sections of time.
Annie Dillard

Great artists treasure
their time with a bitter
and snarling miserliness.
Catherine Drinker Bowen

Take time to deliberate;
but when the time for
action arrives, stop
thinking and go in.
Andrew Jackson

I have always been
a quarter of an hour
before my time, and
it has made a man of me.
Horatio Nelson

I must govern the clock,
not be governed by it.
Golda Meir

May you live all the days of your life.

JONATHAN SWIFT

In Summary: Five Tips for Managing Your Time and Your Life

- Take the time to compose a brief personal mission statement.

- Using your mission statement as a guide, write down a set of clearly defined, measurable goals for the coming year. Review these goals often.

- Start each day with a written to-do list, and prioritize the items on that list. Do the most important tasks first.

- Avoid the habit of mindlessly watching television. There are better things to do with your time and your life.

- Learn to say "no" to things you don't want to do (or don't have time to do). Otherwise, you will allow other people to prioritize your days, your weeks, and, ultimately, your life.

PRINCIPLE #5

Healthy Living

Perhaps you've been taking your health for granted. If so, it's time to take inventory of your life-style.

Good health is viewed by many young people as a natural birthright and a permanent condition. Adults know better. Good health is a gift we give ourselves, a gift that becomes more important as the years pass.

On the pages that follow, we consider the importance of healthy living. Take these words to heart, figuratively *and* literally. After all, you only have one body, and if you don't take care of it, who will?

True enjoyment
comes from activity
of the mind and
exercise of the body:
the two are
ever united.

BARON ALEXANDER
VON HUMBOLDT

Make a commitment
to health and well-being,
and develop a belief in the
possibility of total health.
Bernie Siegel, M.D.

Exercise and physical
fitness can act as
buffers against stress.
Michael H. Sacks, M.D.

People who exercise regularly
have fewer illnesses.
Bernie Siegel, M.D.

We never repent
of having eaten too little.
Thomas Jefferson

Eat to live; do not live to eat.
Poor Richard's Almanac

Moderation is
the secret of survival.
Manly Hall

Everything
in excess is
opposed to
nature.

HIPPOCRATES

The choicest pleasures of life
lie within the ring
of moderation.

Martin Tupper

The healthy, strong individual
is the one who asks for help
when he needs it, whether he
has an abscess on his knee
or in his soul.

Rona Barrett

Happiness is good health and a bad memory.

INGRID BERGMAN

In Summary: Five Tips for Healthy Living

- Find a good healthcare plan and a good general physician.

- Don't overindulge. Moderation leads to happiness and health; overindulgence doesn't.

- If you haven't already done so, begin a regular, sensible exercise program.

- If you don't smoke, don't start. If you do smoke, spend whatever energy and money is required to quit.

- Use sunscreen.

Principle #6

Positive Thinking

Over a lifetime, you'll have plenty of opportunities to become discouraged. Life has a way of handing out occasional disappointments; no one is exempt.

Since life is periodically difficult, you can do yourself a favor by developing the habit of positive thinking. The best time to develop a positive mental attitude is before you need it; consequently, the best day to begin developing a new-found spirit of optimism is today. Then, when trouble rears its ugly head — as it will from time to time — you'll be prepared.

Whenever life throws you a curveball, you have two choices: You can either complain about it — or you can hit it. Your job, of course, is to think good thoughts and keep swinging until you hit a home run.

The mind is like
a clock that
is constantly
running down.
It has to be
wound up
daily with
good thoughts.

BISHOP FULTON J. SHEEN

Success is a state of mind.
If you want success, start
thinking of yourself
as a success.

Dr. Joyce Brothers

Since it doesn't cost a dime
to dream, you'll never
shortchange yourself when
you stretch your imagination.

Robert Schuller

If you think you can, you can.
And if you think you can't,
you're right.

Mary Kay Ash

There are two kinds
of worries — those you can
do something about
and those you can't.
Don't spend any time
on the latter.

Duke Ellington

Keep your fears to yourself,
but share your courage.

Robert Louis Stevenson

Worry and anxiety are
sand in the machinery of life;
faith is the oil.

E. Stanley Jones

Faith is the antiseptic of the soul.

WALT WHITMAN

We must will to be happy
and then work at it.
Alain

The greater part of our
happiness depends on our
disposition and not
our circumstances.
Martha Washington

What happens is not
as important as how you react
to what happens.
Thaddeus Golas

Humor makes
all things possible.
Henry Ward Beecher

Never miss a chance
to laugh out loud.
Douglas Fairbanks, Jr.

Rest and be thankful.
William Wordsworth

Happiness is a habit.
Cultivate it.
Elbert Hubbard

Most people are
about as happy as they make
up their minds to be.
Abraham Lincoln

The longer we dwell
upon our misfortunes,
the greater is their
power to harm us.
Voltaire

Finish every day and be done
with it. You have done what
you could; some blunders and
absurdities have crept in;
forget them as soon
as you can.

Ralph Waldo Emerson

The growth of wisdom
may be gauged accurately by
the decline of ill-temper.

Nietzsche

Anger tortures itself.

Publilius Syrus

An inexhaustible good
nature is one of the most
precious gifts of heaven.
Washington Irving

Laugh and the world laughs
with you. Weep and
you weep alone.
Ella Wheeler Wilcox

I am an optimist.
It does not seem to be
much use being
anything else.
Winston Churchill

Happiness is not a state to arrive at, but a manner of traveling.

SAMUEL JOHNSON

In Summary: Five Tips for Positive Thinking

- Learn to count your blessings, not your troubles. Your troubles are not as great as you might fear, and your blessings are greater than you realize.

- Avoid the habit of blaming others. No one ever wins the blame game, so don't even play.

- Always look for the good in others, especially those closest to you.

- Avoid the natural human tendency of making molehills into mountains.

- Start each day with a few minutes of quiet time to focus your thoughts, to plan your day, and to utter a prayer of gratitude.

PRINCIPLE #7

Living at a Profit

Once you're paying your own way, you'll quickly discover that the old proverb is true: Money doesn't grow on trees. So even if you've got a trust fund *and* a rich uncle, you are well-advised to learn the basic tenets of money management.

Managing money is neither difficult nor complicated. What's required is that you learn to live at a profit by earning more money than you spend. It's as simple as that.

Learning to live within your means is a sign of maturity...and it's also the only sensible way to live.

For some priceless advice about *your* financial future, read on.

Draw your salary
      before spending it.
                      George Ade

Do not count your chickens
      before they hatch.
                      Aesop

Put money in thy purse.
                      Shakespeare

That man is richest whose pleasures are the cheapest.

HENRY DAVID THOREAU

Moderation in all things.

TERENCE

Less is more.

Robert Browning

Any fool can waste, any fool
can muddle, but it takes
something of a man to save.
Rudyard Kipling

The habit of saving is itself
an education; it fosters
every virtue.
T. T. Munger

Save a part of your income
and begin now, for the man
with a surplus controls
circumstances, and the
man without a surplus is
controlled by circumstances.
Henry H. Buckley

What can be added
to the happiness of
a man who is in
health, out of debt,
and has a clear
conscience?

ADAM SMITH

Economy is half
the battle of life;
it is not so hard
to earn money
as it is to
spend it well.

CHARLES SPURGEON

Rule No. 1: Never lose money. Rule No. 2: Never forget rule No. 1.

WARREN BUFFET

In Summary: Five Tips for Living at a Profit

- Avoid credit-card debt at all costs. If you can't afford to pay for it in cash, don't buy it.

- Establish a written budget and live within that budget.

- Spend less than you earn each month.

- Open a retirement account. If your employer matches your contributions to that account, contribute the maximum allowable amount.

- When buying a vehicle, do not go deeply into debt. An expensive monthly car note is the financial equivalent of handcuffs.

PRINCIPLE #8

The Golden Rule

In the New Testament, Jesus advises, "Do unto others as you would have them do unto you." These simple words, when put into practice, form a firm foundation for your dealings with other people.

When you follow the Golden Rule, you treat others honestly and respectfully. When you follow the Golden Rule, you are fair in your dealings, generous with your time, and gentle in your demeanor. When you treat others as you wish to be treated, you feel better about yourself and about your world. Furthermore, you become the kind of person others appreciate and respect.

So the next time you find yourself in a quandary regarding your dealings with another person, ask yourself this question: "How would I want to be treated?" Then do the right thing. The results will be as good as gold.

A friend is a present you give yourself.

ROBERT LOUIS STEVENSON

The best time to make friends is before you need them.

Ethel Barrymore

A faithful friend is a strong defense; and he that hath found him hath found a treasure.

Louisa May Alcott

Become genuinely interested in other people.

Dale Carnegie

Getting people to like you
is merely the other side
of liking them.

Norman Vincent Peale

He who sows courtesy
reaps friendship, and he who
plants kindness gathers love.

Saint Basil

You don't just luck into
things as much as you would
like to think you do. You build
step by step, whether it is
friendships or opportunities.

Barbara Bush

It is wise to apply the oil
of refined politeness to the
mechanism of friendship.

Colette

When someone does
something good, applaud!
You'll make two people happy.

Sam Goldwyn

A man wrapped up in
himself makes a very small
package.

Ben Franklin

Any fool can criticize,
condemn, and complain,
and most fools do.

Dale Carnegie

The best way to have
a friend is to be one.

Ralph Waldo Emerson

Be a friend to yourself, and
others will be too.

Scottish Proverb

All who would win
joy must share it;
happiness was
born a twin.

LORD BYRON

Trickery and treachery
are the practices of fools
who have not wits enough
to be honest.

Ben Franklin

Honest men fear neither
the light nor the dark.

Thomas Fuller

Honesty is the first chapter
in the book of wisdom.

Thomas Jefferson

What you do not want
others to do to you,
do not do to others.

Confucius

You lose a lot of time
hating people.

Marian Anderson

The art of being wise
is knowing what to overlook.

William James

We have committed the
Golden Rule to memory;
let us now commit it
to life.

Edwin Markham

The Golden Rule
is of no use whatsoever
unless you realize that
it is your move.

DR. FRANK CRANE

<u>In Summary: Five Tips for Living the Golden Rule</u>

- Be kind to everyone you meet, even to those people who don't return your kindness.

- Develop a reputation for honesty and integrity; be honest, even when you must tell people things they don't want to hear.

- When in doubt, follow your conscience; do the right thing, not the expedient thing.

- Be quick to forgive everyone, starting with yourself.

- If you're married, make your marriage an ultimate priority in your life.

Principle #9

Abundant Living

Graduation is now but a memory, and the rest of your life beckons. And what a life it can be *if* you approach each day with a sense of celebration.

But beware: If you allow fears and regrets to rule your thoughts, you will experience predictably poor results.

So make this post-graduation resolution: Resolve to live abundantly, thankfully, and expectantly. Make your life a series of one-day celebrations.

Give thanks for your blessings and enjoy every step of your journey, realizing that each day holds its own unique treasures, but realizing too that those treasures are not yours until you claim them.

A man is never old until
regrets take the place
of his dreams.

John Barrymore

No matter how long you live,
die young.

Elbert Hubbard

Whether it's the best of
times, or the worst of times,
it's the only time you've got.

Art Buchwald

Life is a journey,
not a destination.
Happiness is not
"there," but here,
not tomorrow,
but today.

SIDNEY GREENBERG

Life is in the living, in
the tissue of every day
and hour.

Stephen Leacock

Live with no time out.

Simone de Beauvoir

Plunge boldly into
the thick of life!

Goethe

Begin to live
at once, and
count each day a
separate life.

SENECA

Dost thou love life?
Then do not squander time,
    for that's the stuff
    life is made of.
                    Ben Franklin

The passing minute is
every man's equal possession.
                    Marcus Aurelius

Nobody's gonna live for you.
                    Dolly Parton

We find in life exactly
what we put into it.
Ralph Waldo Emerson

Life is what we make it.
Always has been.
Always will be.
Grandma Moses

Live out your life in its
full meaning. It is God's life.
Josiah Royce

Never run out of goals.

Earl Nightingale

The greatest use of a life
is to spend it for something
that will outlast it.

William James

Life is either a daring
adventure or nothing.

Helen Keller

Assume
responsibility
for the quality
of your own life.

NORMAN COUSINS

Nothing in life is to be
feared. It is only to be
understood.

Marie Curie

Alas! The fearful unbelief
is unbelief in yourself.

Thomas Carlyle

My recipe for life is
not being afraid of myself.

Eartha Kitt

He knows not his own
strength that has not
met adversity.

Ben Johnson

We cannot learn
without pain.

Aristotle

There is no education
like adversity.

Benjamin Disraeli

The tragedy of life is not so much what men suffer as what they miss.

THOMAS CARLYLE

When life kicks you,
    let it kick you forward.

E. Stanley Jones

Begin to weave, and
    God will give the thread.

German Proverb

Do not take life too
seriously. You'll never get
    out of it alive.

Elbert Hubbard

Make your life a mission — not an intermission.

ARNOLD GLASGOW

Find the
journey's end in
every step.

RALPH WALDO EMERSON

In Summary: Five Tips for Abundant Living

- Take time each day to pause and give thanks for the life you've been given.

- Live in the present. Don't fret too much about yesterday or worry too much about tomorrow. Do your best today, and leave the rest up to God.

- Accept responsibility for the quality of your life. If something in your life needs doing, don't wait for someone else to step in and do it for you; do it yourself.

- Never let past failures keep you from following your dreams.

- Remember that when all is said and done, your happiness depends, first and foremost, upon you.

Sources

Sources

About the Author

Criswell Freeman is a Doctor of Clinical Psychology living in Nashville, Tennessee. He is the author of *When Life Throws You a Curveball, Hit It* and numerous other books including *The Wisdom Series* from Walnut Grove Press. Dr. Freeman is also the host of the nationally syndicated radio program *Wisdom Made in America*.

About
DELANEY STREET PRESS

DELANEY STREET PRESS publishes books designed to inspire and entertain readers of all ages. DELANEY STREET books are distributed by WALNUT GROVE PRESS. For more information, call 1-800-256-8584.

*If you enjoyed this book,
you're sure to enjoy other titles
from Delaney Street Press.
For more information,
please call:*

1-800-256-8584